Preface

I hope you find within these pages something uniquely helpful towards becoming a more successful debater and an overall clearer thinker. It is meant as a needed resource for both students and coaches who want to learn more about LD debate. If you find this helpful and useful, or have any kind of critical feedback please email me at griffith.ben@att.net. I am more than willing to answer questions, clarify something I have said in this book, or correct any mistakes (of which I'm sure there will be plenty). I also put on workshops and help research and write cases for LD debaters. If you're interested in any coaching/case-writing services contact me and I would love to partner with you in becoming a more successful high school debater.

Why I wrote this book...

It was only a few years ago that I was a freshman in high school with an interest in joining the debate team. I borrowed an upperclassman's cases, bought a cheap suit, got a 45 minute crash course on how a LD round worked, ... and I was off!

By a pure stroke of fortune (drawing two people who were as lost as I was), I tasted the sweetness of success and finished in the top 16 of a tournament with over a hundred debaters. All it took was that one experience to implant a passion (some would say addiction) for high school debate.

So for three years, I made use of every resource I could find to become a better debater. I spent hours on online forums and tried my best to grow as a debater by reading our dated textbooks and philosopher wikipedia articles. One summer I even attended a week-long debate camp.

But what I never found was a readable guide to becoming a successful debater.

So, the idea for this book was born. This book is an attempt at a short, readable, understandable guide for both students and teachers in Lincoln-Douglas debate. While there are several *textbook style* debate books that serve as well as a fourth leg to an old couch as learning to debate, and there are quality debate camps that can cost upwards of $500–to my knowledge there's not a concise and affordable explanation of the most important aspects of LD debate. So, this book is an **introduction** for debaters who want to have a solid grasp of LD.

By "introduction" I have in mind someone who already has a general understanding of the basics of LD Debate– perhaps a freshman who has already participated in a tournament or two, or has at least competed in some practice rounds at school. If you are BRAND NEW to LD, I have made an effort to explain everything in a way that will be understandable. If there is something you don't understand, google it, or just read on and it will become clearer after reading the entire book. I also have envisioned this book as something that should be read multiple times as you grow as a debater. Try to understand as much as possible, but also know that this book will be more and more helpful as you progressively have more experience debating.

But, this is also meant to be **more than just an introduction**. Now that I completed an undergrad degree in philosophy and am well into a graduate degree in theology, I understand the extreme value in learning the skills that LD teaches. And this is the second major reason I wanted to write this book: **learning to be a good LD debater is about learning to be a good *thinker***. I want to push readers—whether you're just beginning or are a fourth year varsity debater—to not only be able to win rounds, but to learn how to engage in fruitful and productive dialogue. The skill of weighing ideas humbly and respectfully with those whom you disagree is the most enduring lesson that high school debate can teach.

The book is divided into two sections. Section 1 is devoted to more general or theoretical areas that are vital to becoming a more successful LD debater. Chapter 1 will answer the question: "What is Philosophy?" including the massive confusion around the difference between policy debate and value/philosophy debate. Chapter 2 will look at the Value/Criterion relationship. Just as there is mass confusion when it comes to understanding what "philosophy" means, there is perhaps even MORE confusion about the role of the criterion. If you can only understand and implement the value/criterion relationship as described in this chapter, you will be hard pressed to ever lose another round. In Chapter 3 we will address the important-yet-overlooked topic of the "Ethics of Debate." What if our debates looked more like a generous conversation than trench warfare? The most important lesson to be learned from any form of high school debate is how to engage in healthy dialogue with another person who has a differing opinion.

Section 2 will then move beyond these general ideas towards concrete advice on case-writing, some guidance on speaking and an overview what a debater should accomplish in each speech in the round, and finally a chapter devoted to "flowing." Section 2 will be as practical as Section 1 is theoretical–it will contain suggestions that are directly transferable into a debate round.

Section 1

General Ideas You Need to Know

Chapter 1: Philosophy

What exactly does a Lincoln-Douglas debater do? In short, LD competitors engage in philosophical debate and discussion. Each LD resolution poses a philosophical question about a contemporary topic. The debate topic may force you to explore questions such as: the ethics of torture in military operations, the future of space exploration programs, high school drug testing, or foreign policies. All of these issues are addressed from a *philosophical* standpoint. But *what* exactly is philosophy?

From high school debate, through undergrad, and now into grad school I have heard dozens of different definitions and explanations of the task of philosophy. For philosophical debate like LD, the best definition of philosophy is:

Phi•los•o•phy [n.]: deep, well-reasoned thought and argumentation about a complex issue.

This is precisely what a philosopher is called to do. Whether a high school debater or the chair of the philosophy department at Harvard, a philosopher's task is to think deeply in an attempt to provide some understanding for the complex questions in the human experience.

Depending on who you ask, there are several classical areas or "branches" of philosophy. Logic, Epistemology, Metaphysics, Aesthetics, and Axiology are commonly identified as "The Five Branches of Philosophy"; but within these you have the Philosophy of Religion, Philosophy of Science, and Ethics (including philosophical ethics, theological ethics, bio-ethics, sexual ethics, political ethics etc.). By just picking up an introductory textbook to philosophy or looking up the wikipedia article, the breadth of philosophy can be completely overwhelming.

Of all of the above topics, the most important for LD debate is the area on which almost every topic focuses—**ethics**. Other than a Fall topic from a few years back that involved space exploration (which is probably nearer to Philosophy of Science than political ethics), every topic I've debated, judged, or found on the internet involves ethics.

Within ethics, the most notable philosophers are those that are mentioned year after year in LD cases: Kant, Mill, Hobbes, Locke, and Rawls. You will go a long way in developing as a debater if you begin by reading some secondary literature (like Bertrand Russell's *A History of Western Philosophy* or a shorter book like Rachels's *The Elements of Moral Philosophy*) on these thinkers or even just the Wikipedia and online encyclopedia articles. But don't stop there. Find primary works that you can read, especially of English speaking philosophers like Mill,

Locke, and Rawls. Reading the primary literature will grow you as a writer, a thinker, a debater, and as a student in general. We will return to how to use philosophers in the round in the case-writing chapter. But, for now, the point is to take the time to really *learn* philosophical ethics, don't just tack a name on your case so you sound smart.

Part of defining Lincoln-Douglas debate (as a form of value/philosophy debate) is by describing how it differs from policy debate (such as CX debate).

Forget everything you've ever heard about the differences between philosophy (or value) debate and policy debate. If I judge 100 rounds of LD, in at least 50 of them I will hear this phrase: "this is value debate, not policy, so your argument doesn't matter." And CX debaters are just as guilty. Although it happens less, you will hear a CXer say that an argument isn't valid because it is philosophical rather than evidential. So let's put this confusion to rest.

When we are talking about the difference between policy and value debate, we are talking about the different aims of policy-making and philosophical theorizing. So in order to understand the policy/value distinction, imagine the different roles of a politician (a policy maker) and a professor of philosophical ethics (a philosopher). The politician is responsible for writing a concrete policy that involves an assessment of the current situation, feasibility of success, enforcement when someone violates the policy, and many other factors that involve the concrete situation in which the policy is to be enacted. The professor, on the other hand, has the luxury of not having to account for all of on-the-ground issues of making a certain policy work– instead, he is responsible for asking questions of whether a policy *ought* to be done.

I think a couple examples here would be helpful. First, consider the War in Iraq. The policy-makers, Barack Obama and his staff, are responsible for determining policies for military action that include budgetary concerns, foreign affairs and number of active military personnel (these types of concerns fit within the traditional CX "stock issues" of solvency, harms and inherency). But, while Barack Obama is given the difficult task of actually constructing a military policy that will work out all of the details of its effectiveness, the philosopher is only concerned with whether the action *ought* to be done. And further, a philosopher is concerned with the action of "war" itself, not only the morality of the specific historical event of the War in Iraq. The philosopher would consider the field of philosophical ethics, the tradition of Just War, and the many philosophers who have reflected and contributed to our collective understanding of the justice (or injustice) of war. University ethicists and theologians then indirectly contribute to policies by writing articles and contributing to political think-tanks in an attempt for the political institution to listen to their ethical reflection. The policy-making and the philosophizing have definite overlap, but their are still very distinct enterprises.

A second example. Another controversial political issue is the current American debate on gay marriage. This single political issue involves both (1) determining if gay marriage as a social institution is beneficial to American society and (2) whether gay marriage is *good* or *right*. Clearly there is some overlap–the most popular argument against gay marriage as a beneficial social institution is in fact a moral argument. The Religious Right claims that *since* gay marriage is evil, it would be a detriment to American society. But notice that the two issues, while similar, are also very different. Some people argue that gay marriage is *wrong*, but that as a civil institution it is perfectly valid. Others argue that gay marriage is *good*, but that there are too many unresolvable social issues that the legalization of gay marriage would create. Each concern– that of policymaking and that of ethics–has its own set of aims and questions.

These two examples provide a few points about the difference between philosophical reflection and policy-making: **One, philosophical reflection is not context specific**. This point is huge, because I hear confusion on this point in almost every round on every topic.

Determining whether or not gay marriage is *justified* is not a solely or uniquely American issue. Obviously, answering that question is going to have an effect on the types of policies that we create in America, but answering whether gay marriage is moral or ethical has little to do with the current political debates in America. When you address a LD resolution, you are in a sense answering this question for all people everywhere, it is a universal decision. Debaters who I judged during the Spring 2011 topic on the foreign trade policies of Free Trade vs. Protectionism drove me crazy because almost every round included an argument concerning whether the United States's foreign policy is free trade or protectionist. And every time I heard that argument, I sat and thought, "this has absolutely no relevance to determining what should be valued higher." Philosophy is about determining what *ought* to be done, not what *is* already going on.

Two, philosophical reflection precedes, and is a part of, policymaking. While philosophical musing is not context specific (e.g. determining the morality of gay marriage), it must be done before policies can be made, and it influences the types of policies that come into existence. This is the reason why it actually is ok to make a ethical or philosophical argument in a policy debate. I honestly want to know what a CXer who claims that philosophy doesn't have a role in policy debate would say about the institution of slavery. The abolition of slavery is a clear historical example of how a nation (or at least half of it) realized that policies needed to change because they were unethical, despite their economic fruitfulness. Value debate is a heightened reflection on one of the many aspects that go into policymaking.

Three, **Policymaking involves weighing and working through many more contingencies than philosophical reflection**. This doesn't mean that philosophy is any easier than policymaking, in fact I believe that philosophy is much more difficult because it is so much more abstract. In policy debate (like CX), the affirmative offers a plan to create a new policy that includes how it is to be implemented, what is going to take place, where the funding will come from, how it will solve current problems, and why those problems are not already being solved. A policy debate HAS to go through all of that because their resolution calls for them to actually do something in the real world and show that the world would be a better place as a result. Philosophical reflection, however, does not have to answer ANY of those questions, because for something to be good or just, it doesn't necessarily have to be implementable in our contemporary American society.This is evidenced by my earlier example of those who think that gay marriage is just and good, but feel that as a social policy it would be destructive. Another way of putting this is that policy debate is much more *realist*, while value debate is more *idealist*. Philosophy debates the ideals (what is the best option in the perfect world), whereas policy debates realistic circumstances (what is the best *possible* option in the current world that we have).

As a final attempt to spell out this difference, here is a pair of contrasting resolutions.

Policy Resolution: "The United States Federal Government should adopt a Free Trade foreign policy."

Value Resolution: "Free Trade ought to be valued above Protectionism."

This pair of resolutions displays the different set of aims and questions that comes with either policy or value debate. In the first, there is a specific agent (the United States federal Government) and a specific action (adopt policies). However, the second resolution (which was UIL's Spring 2011 topic) has neither a specific agent nor a specific action. It is merely asking a value question about these two political doctrines for foreign affairs. While real world examples can help clarify the terms of the resolution, telling me how well Free Trade or Protectionism has worked in the real world doesn't necessarily exhibit which should be valued more. Likewise, telling me that America is Free Trade does not mean that it's more valuable either, since just because America is democratic or Free Trade (or whatever else) does not necessarily imply that it those characteristics are valuable (even though we live here).

Far too often I sit in an LD round and feel like the debate has turned into a policy debate about the first resolution example. When you hear an opponent of yours trying to make policy-type arguments, call them on it.

Finally, **a short word about argumentation**. Philosophy is argumentation. Philosophy is the ability to think through an idea, consider all of it's sides and angles, and then articulate your ideas in a way that is understandable. Therefore, being able to argue analytically is absolutely vital to debate.

Learning to argue and think critically is one of the most important qualities of a good debater, and–as it turns out–it is the hardest to teach. Very often, critical thinking is something that takes many years to develop. In my experience, debate is an activity that is best suited for naturally inquisitive people who also enjoy thinking through difficult ideas and expressing their opinions.

There are so, so many resources (and many of them free) for argumentation–find one and just go chapter by chapter through the exercises. The ability to read and interpret texts, listen to arguments, and think on your feet are both important as a debater and will help you so much throughout your life regardless of your career. Sometimes I wonder if a show like *The O'Reilly Factor* would even exist if the general public understood sound argumentation. Become a debater who wins based on an attitude of inquisitive learning rather than O'Reilly-style bullying.

Chapter 2: The Value/Criterion Relationship

This chapter is the most important in this book. If you can understand the value/criterion relationship in an LD case, then you will be well on your way to win a lot of rounds.

Here is the anatomy of a Lincoln-Douglas case:

Every case has a value, a criterion, and one or more contentions. The **value** is a concept that we find highly valuable. Your value could be a number of things: justice, peace, security, love, self-actualization, etc.

The **criterion** is usually defined as a standard that *achieves* or *defines* the value. In the criterion, we have stumbled upon an aspect of LD that is extremely misunderstood. In a moment, we will look in depth at the flaws in the common (mis)understanding of the criterion, but for now I'm going to introduce a unique take on the criterion that I find much more plausible and philosophically sound. **The criterion is a philosophical theory or doctrine that guarantees the value and renders the resolution either true or false.** Let's unpack this ...

Let's say that I am the affirmative debater on the Spring 2011 UIL Topic: "Free Trade ought to be valued above Protectionism." My value is equality, and my criterion is J.S. Mill's Utilitarianism (which basically says that it is ethical to pursue the action that creates the greatest good for the greatest number of people). I would argue that my criterion (Mill's Utilitarianism) guarantees the value (equality) and renders the resolution (that Free Trade ought to be valued above Protectionism) as true. By structuring a case this way, there is a very clear line of reasoning. Value is good therefore the criterion is good therefore the resolution is true/justified (or false if you're the negative debater).

As we will see later, case-writing becomes very easy once you find that philosophical theory or doctrine that upholds or denies the resolution. Your contention(s) will simply explain that logical order, defend your criterion, and explain why the criterion is relevant to the topic at hand. But the key is finding that criterion and learning it well enough so that you know more about it than your opponent and are prepared for all of the potential objections to it.

Now that we have positively defined the value and criterion, let's take a look at the most common flaws in a Value/Criterion (these terms originally came from a workshop with James Willis):

First, **Value/Criterion Circularity**. The debater is guilty of circularity when the value depends upon the criterion and the criterion depends on the value. Sometimes a student will offer the value of justice and the criterion of fairness. If you ask when justice is met, they will answer "fairness," and if you ask when fairness is met, they will respond "justice." Clearly, in such a case, nothing is actually being proven, and they have a case that is purely circular.

Second, **Insufficient Criterion**. Because your value is what makes the criterion *valuable*, the criterion must be able to guarantee the value–it must be sufficient within itself to create the value. For example, sometimes you will see a case with a criterion of safety and a value of liberty. In this example, for the criterion to be sufficient then safety would always have to sufficiently cause liberty. Clearly, though, there are times when a person is perfectly safe but does not have liberty. An absurd example can show this well: imagine a person locked inside a padded jail cell–they could not be any safer, yet they have no liberty.

Third, **Biased Criterion or Value**. This flaw is another example of circular reasoning. Sometimes you will find debaters who use one of the terms in the resolution as their value or criterion. For example, I heard several cases with a value of Free Trade in the topic: "Free Trade ought to be valued above Protectionism." In essence, this person is arguing: "Free Trade ought to be valued because of Free Trade." And that is circular.

Fourth, **Criterion Begging**. This is by far the most chronic problem among LDers. A criterion is begging when it is in need of another criterion. As stated earlier, the criterion creates, causes, or results in the value. But often the criterion is in need of another criterion. With a value of Justice and a criterion of Safety, even if you could show that justice is met, Safety needs its own criterion to show when Safety is met. This is why I believe it is so vital to have a philosophical theory or doctrine as a criterion. With something like Mill's Utilitarianism, your criterion is substantial enough to support your value without needing any further criteria.

These are four terms that you need to memorize because

you will be able to use them in many debate rounds. In two years of LD debating when I was in High School, I was able to point out one of these four flaws in dozens of rounds in invitational tournaments. Even if your judge doesn't have a clue about the *proper role of the value and criterion* in that last speech when you say: "my opponent's criterion needs another criterion!" you can get them smiling and nodding as they sign your name on the ballot.

Whenever your opponent reads their value and criterion, your first reaction should be to run through these four flaws in your head, asking if they are guilty of one or more of them. If so, this will be your biggest attack on their case, because without a sound value and criterion, your opponent's case does not have a chance of affirming or negating the resolution.

In summary, in this understanding of an LD case, the criterion is the most important part of the argument. The criterion is valuable because it simultaneously creates the value (justice, peace, security, etc.), and either affirms of denies the resolution. Because the criterion has to function this way in order for the resolution to be affirmed (as I have argued in this chapter), the only adequate criterion is a philosophical theory or doctrine. I will go on to show how this plays out in an entire case in the chapter on case-writing.

Chapter 3: Ethics of Debate

I believe in a world where people can disagree in faith and politics, yet still get along.

I know that's a radical idea, and one that is about as likely as Palestinians and Jews dropping their guns, high fiving, and calling it even–but reasonable, humble dialogue is still a goal that I think is worth working towards.

In LD debate, as with any kind of debate, participants have a choice between two attitudes or dispositions. The first is that of a generous conversation, perhaps even between two friends, who are seeking to discover new insights to a complex question. The second is like trench warfare.

This is an area where our contemporary American politics have failed us. Another election season means another round of vitriol ("mudslinging" in *lehman's terms*). Every day I can read or watch political news and find another *stand-off* between Republicans and Democrats. Both sides have their own wishes and neither is willing to budge– which I understand; but neither is willing to have a civil conversation either–which I DON'T understand. (I think of a local political candidate's ad commercial that asks, "is this *really* the time to be reaching across the aisle?" Yes... Yes it is.)

So take this word of advice: **please treat the debate round more like conversation over a cup of coffee with your friend than the Hot Seat in the O'Reilly Factor.** No matter how often we see political or religious leaders choosing to shout at one another rather than converse, it's perfectly fine to break the trend. So when you're in a round, don't be a jerk. It doesn't help you win rounds; in fact, more often than not it turns judges off. But more than that, it should be a life lesson: humble people who are willing to listen to others and take other's opinions seriously are better learners.

In the round, be a student. Listen to what they're saying and treat the other debater with respect. If you will do this, then the skill of weighing ideas humbly and respectfully with those who you disagree with is the most enduring lesson that high school debate can teach.

Section 2

Competing in Debate: From Researching to Rebuttals

Chapter 4: Case-Writing

Case writing is the most fun part of LD debate. The case is the one tangible artifact that you can look at and know that you have accomplished something. After a round is over, you have a scribbled "flow" of arguments and notes from the round, but the case is the foundation of your argument, and it is the only speech that you know you have total control over. This chapter will build on the earlier chapter about the value/criterion relationship to show how you actually put this into practice. This chapter will address both the issue of case writing and the importance of researching your topic. For the sake of this chapter, I am going to model how to write a case based on the resolution we have mentioned several times: "Free Trade ought to be valued above Protectionism."

When I see this particular topic, the **first thing I want to do is make sure I understand all of the terms involved in the resolution**. In this case, its is fairly clear that the issue at hand is between a foreign policy that allows free trading between nations and one that blocks off trade from other nations for the purpose of protecting one's own political interests. Because this is a hot button issue in contemporary politics (as most resolutions will be), the best way of understanding the issue is by searching the library for a book about foreign trade policies. Your research on this front will be the best resource for definitions that you can include in the beginning of your case.

Once we have nailed down the scope of the topic and understand what issue it is referring to, it is time to become a philosopher. Since the topic addresses which of two foreign political policies *ought* to be *valued*, I know that it is an issue of political ethics. So my first move is to begin thinking about how various ethicists would address this issue. What would Kant think about this resolution? What would Rawls think about this resolution? What about Mill, Locke, or Hobbes? Maybe even the writings of the ancient philosopher Aristotle, or the 20th century author and economist Ayn Rand could speak to this topic. By using these thinkers as a starting point, I can find an argument that I find plausible and defensible that is also a coherent and respected political philosophy. This is probably the hardest part of the case-writing process because it is not easy to become acquainted with all of these different philosophers, and many of the "popular level" resources are not very good–and by *not good*, I mean, never read them because they will only confuse you. Try to find someone who has studied philosophy or, at the least, read a secondary source like Russell's *A History of Western Philosophy*. It is better to put in the work to have a good understanding of a few philosophers, than to be totally confused and misinformed about many. Also, there are people available who perform workshops to explain philosophy for a given topic. If you're interested in something like this, check out my contact info on the first page.

Often, if you find one philosopher that you really resonate with and you learn everything you can about that one figure, then you can write a case on just about any topic from their philosophical perspective. I knew of one girl who enjoyed the work of Ayn Rand, so every year at least one of her two cases was an Ayn Rand case. This is a way that you can limit the amount of research you have to do, and still have a really good knowledge of at least one classical philosopher.

Once you have found your philosopher, you have found your criterion. The next step is to write your case around this criterion. After I have understood the topic of Free Trade vs. Protectionism, and have researched and thought through some philosophical perspectives, I decide to write my affirmative case based on Mill's Utilitarianism. This means that my value will be equality and my criterion is Mill's Utilitarianism. For this particular case, I read widely enough to understand what Mill's Utilitarianism involves. I start by reading an online encyclopedia for J. S. Mill, then read the wikipedia article, but then I do the important work of buying Mill's book entitled *Utilitarianism*. The book is very readable and it's only about 70 pages. Any high schooler could read it in one sitting.

Each criterion is going to have a natural value that grows from it. In the case of Mill's Utilitarianism, the value is going to be equality. Mill's theory is based on the notion of creating equality of pleasure for the greatest number of people. Your value is what makes the criterion *valuable*, but is also your common ground between you, your opponent, and the judge. Everyone in the room values equality, so that is how you convince the judge that your case should win, and that your case is better than that of your opponent. "If we can all agree that equality is valuable," you would say, "then Mill's Utilitarianism is a valuable criterion."

The next task is to **determine how Utilitarianism relates to the resolution**. Obviously, you have already been thinking about this–it's the reason that you chose the criterion in the first place. When researching the philosophers, our guiding question was: "What would _____ think about the resolution?" So now that we have found a philosopher in J. S. Mill who it seems would be a defender of Free Trade over Protectionism it is time to spell this out in detail. **Relating the criterion to the resolution is the single task of your contention(s)**.

Most LD Cases have between 2 and 4 contentions. I think this is a mistake. Compiling a list of contentions seems like a tactic in hiding the fact that you have no clue what you are arguing for. I am a big believer in **one contention cases**. And I believe that the best formula for your one and only contention is to word it:

According to [criterion], [resolution].

Or, if you are the negative: According to [criterion], NOT [resolution].

So in this sample case we are constructing, your one contention would be: "According to Mill's Utilitarianism, Free Trade ought to be valued above Protectionism"; or if you were writing the negative case on this topic, you would say, "According to [criterion], Free Trade ought NOT to be valued above Protectionism." In this one simple sentence, you have summarized your entire case and argument. And simple, summary sentences are easy to sell to a judge in that last speech.

With this contention tagline, you should add several sub points that explain *why* your criterion shows the resolution as true/justified or false. Included in the sub points should be preemptive responses to common objections. As you debate your case, take note of the most difficult objections that other debaters argue, and then go ahead and write preemptive responses to those objections into your case for the next tournament. In this sample case, I'd go with:

Sub Point A: Mill's Utilitarianism can function as a political ethic for international policy.

Sub Point B: Free Trade Promotes equal quality of pleasures for more people.

Sub Point C: Protectionism destroys equality and puts the interests of a single nation above the collective interests of all people.

Under each sub point, you are going to write several paragraphs defending why you believe each of those statements to be true. It is even appropriate to bring in some real world evidence of how Free Trade promotes equality. I find historical examples extremely helpful in trying to give evidence for your perspective on the terms of the resolution.

And you're done. You have constructed a case with a very simple logical flow that is also very compelling and rational. You defend your criterion based on the value that it creates, then you show how your criterion renders the resolution either true or false. If your arguments in the case are good and you have chosen a good criterion, winning or losing the round will simply boil down to how well you can explain this to the judge.

Case-writing process checklist:

1.   Understand major issues involved in the resolution.

2.   Identify what area of philosophy the resolution fits within (most likely political ethics)

3.   Identify philosophical arguments ("what would _____ say?") that either affirm or negate the resolution.

4.   Once you find the argument, make that philosophical doctrine your criterion.

5.   Attach the value that your criterion creates—this is your common ground to argue why your criterion should be accepted as normative.

6.   Construct your contention to connect the criterion to the resolution.

Chapter 5: In the Round

Now that we have discussed how to write the all-important cases that will serve as the basis of all of your in-round arguments, we now turn what will actually take place in your debate round. We will first discuss some skills that you will need that have nothing to do with how well you reason or argue.

Since my main reason for writing this book is to help with the reasoning, philosophy, and argumentation aspects of LD Debate, I will only briefly discuss the importance of your speaking ability. Often, speech teachers who coach debate are your best resource for this part of debate, so take advantage of using your current teachers or coaches for your speaking skills. After these general comments, I will then go speech-by-speech through a debate round and tell you exactly what you should accomplish during each speech.

Here is some general advice about the speaking aspect of debate.

Never look at your opponent during Cross Examination. Just don't do it. I know that it's tempting, especially since you are talking to them, but it looks bad and you are more likely to say something really mean. Just keep your eyes forward looking and speaking to the judge when you are asking or answering questions.

Always wear nice clothes. Don't wear tennis shoes, t-shirts, or even collared pull overs. Wear something that looks very professional. It will tell the judge that you are taking debate very seriously, and it will actually help your mentality in the round. I used to think it was cool or edgy to be the guy who dresses down; but it's not. It's dumb.

Giving advice about speaking style is difficult because different judges and different types of debate have such different opinions about the appropriate speaking style. So, the best advice is to know what your judge wants. Speak at a fast rate, but one that is still understandable and a rate that you can be persuasive. Don't waste any time by speaking slowly, but remember that your greatest goal is to convince the judge of the validity of your criterion and your one contention. So speak clearly, don't let your body movements be distractive, and look your judge in the eyes when you are trying to sway them to your perspective.

One more word about judges, you need to learn how to *read* your judge. When I judge a round, I hear and understand a lot more than the high school science teacher that got pulled into judging at the last second. Don't assume that your judge will completely comprehend what you're talking about—and especially don't assume that they understand aspects of debate such as the value/criterion relationship that you learned in this book. They won't understand it. But it is your job to explain your case, and argue against your opponents flaws in such a way that you make them understand. It is really unfortunate when a debater had better arguments, better reasons, better understanding, yet lost the round because they were not convincing to a judge.

So, when you enter the room to debate ALWAYS ask the judge for a paradigm. If they have no clue what you're talking about, assume that you are going to have to do a lot of simplifying and explaining in the round. If they do have a paradigm, listen to what they say, but don't trust that they will actually judge based on what they have said. Often a judge will feel less embarrassed if they rattle off some "smart-sounding" paradigm even though they don't have a clue what they are looking for. The best policy is to read the judge's face throughout the round, try to discern whether they are tracking with your arguments or if they are having a hard time comprehending you. In the end, stray on the side of simplification.

Now, for a speech by speech breakdown of what you should accomplish and how you should handle your time in each speech. Timing is very important so ALWAYS carry a stopwatch with you so you can monitor your own time.

Affirmative Constructive (AC) – 6 Minutes

The AC is the simplest speech of all. Hopefully you have written a good, solid case that you feel comfortable with. When you write your case, take advantage of having six full minutes. Don't get up and read your case in four minutes, make use of the entire time.

Cross Examination (CX) – 3 Minutes

Most beginner debaters love the CX speech, because it is your chance to address your opponent directly. Many debaters I have judged seem to think this time is an opportunity to get into a verbal altercation with their opponent, or as a time to make the other student look like an idiot.

Against these less than ideal pursuits, your CX time, whether Affirmative or Negative, should have one goal and one goal only: **to clarify confusion and gain understanding of your opponent's case.**

If you sense there is an issue with the relationship of your opponent's value, criterion, and contentions, ask questions about how they relate to one another:

- "Explain your Value to me in your own words..."
- "How does your criterion relate to your value?"
- "How does your contention(s) relate to your V/C"
- "How does your criterion relate to the resolution?"

-      "Why have you included Contention 2?"

But in all of these questions, keep your tone neutral and inquisitive. Act as though you are genuinely interested in hearing their answers and explanations. Chances are, many cases you run up against are not going to be as logically tight as yours if you follow the earlier suggestions in this book. But sometimes your opponent will answer their questions well. And sometimes, you may face another debater whose case is just as logically coherent as your own. In this case, you are going to have a very good and fruitful debate round because you are going to have to defend the merits of your own criterion over that of your opponent.

Negative Constructive (NC) – 7 Minutes

The NC should be split in half into essentially two speeches. In your first 3:30, read your Negative case. When writing the Negative case, limit the length so that you can read it in 3:00–3:30 so that you have ample time to argue against the Affirmative case (have that stopwatch with you so you can monitor your time).

Once you have read your case, go down the Affirmative flow, line-by-line (I will explain how to flow in the final chapter–if you are completely unfamiliar with the concept of flowing, it might be helpful to read that before continuing this chapter). You want to address EVERY part of the Affirmative case. Look for flaws in their V/C relationship that were elucidated during your CX time. Seek logical inconsistencies between their contention(s) and their overall argument. Show why your case is more logically consistent and viable than your opponents.

All of your arguments should be pre-written down during your "prep time" between the CX and your next speech, so that the speech is merely you reading and explaining your answers to the judge. Use your prep time wisely so that you are doing as little thinking "on the fly" as possible.

Cross Examination (CX) – 3 Minutes

After the NC, the Affirmative then has the opportunity to cross examine the Negative. Use the same guidelines offered above–seek understanding, don't make arguments.

First Affirmative Rebuttal (1AR) – 4 Minutes

The 1AR and 2AR speeches are equally difficult to navigate. There is a ton to cover, and not very much time to do it.

The only way to cover everything, and still have time to convince the judge that you should win the round is to use the 1AR as a time to go down the flow line-by-line, and then the 2AR is completely dedicated to synthesizing the round and giving definitive reasons why you won.

So, in the 1AR, spend the first 2 minutes going through the Negative case raising objections to their constructive argument, then spend 2 minutes going down your flow answering all of the objections raised by the negative during the NC.

This is a hard-hitting, rapid fire style where you need to establish all of the main arguments in the round. You have to lay the ground work for your next speech when you will break down the round, weigh the arguments, and tell the judge why you have won the round. Again, use your "prep time" before this speech to write out all of your arguments against your opponent. Try to find unique, analytically sound arguments against each point of their case. Then respond to the objections they have raised. If you know your case well, and your criterion well, then responding to objections will be a piece of cake.

Negative Rebuttal (NR) – 6 Minutes

The NR is a fun speech because you get to go down the flow AND give your reasons for winning the round. During your "prep time" before this speech, in addition to writing out your arguments for each case, write a list of 2–5 "voters"–concrete reasons why you have won the round.

Always give at least two and never more than five voters. Voters will greatly improve your chances of winning the round because you have just given the judge several concise reasons that they can write down for voting for you.

Spend the first 4–5 minutes going down the flow, building on all of the arguments that you made during the 1NC. Begin by going down the flow on your own case, responding to any arguments or objections that the Affirmative has raised. Then, go down the Affirmative case, reiterating the arguments you made earlier and responding to the Affirmative rebuttal.

In the last 1–2 minutes, put down the flow and give several voters for why you have won the round. If you can't come up with a few good reasons why you have won the round, then chances are, the judge isn't going to be able to either. Make the ballot decision easy for the judge by giving her concise and compelling reasons why you have won the round based on the key arguments that have surfaced during the round. Refer to my advice on the 2AR below for more help with voters.

Second Affirmative Rebuttal (2AR) – 3 Minutes

In many rounds, by the 2AR, the judge has already made up his mind who he will be voting for. However, in close rounds, the advantage goes to the Affirmative because you have the final chance to sway the judge with one compelling speech.

The 2AR should be treated like a summary of the round from your perspective, which is obviously biased towards your arguments. Jettison the flow. That's right, you have already made all of those arguments in the 1AR, and by this time all of the back and forth between you and your opponent has gone on long enough. The judge is ready for you to put down your flow sheet and stare her in the eyes and give a summary of the round.

This formula can be tweaked according to how you feel

about it, but a safe rule of thumb is to break up the 2AR into one minute describing your opponents case, one minute describing your case, and the final minute offering a synthesis that includes your 2–5 voters (again, it is paramount that you have your own stopwatch so that you can closely monitor your time).

In that first minute, nutshell what your opponent is *trying* to do with their case. Don't immediately rebut their case, but frame it in a way that makes clear their cases deficiencies. If their criterion is begging, describe it as if it is begging. If their contentions are contradictory or don't make sense, describe them in a way that they don't make sense. But, in this description, be generous to your opponent's case and their key arguments. Misrepresenting your opponent's case to make it look worse than it is will be obvious to a judge, and it may even cause you to lose the round.

In the next minute, give a concise summary of your case. Every single round, begin your summary by stating: "The resolution is affirmed according to [criterion]. The criterion is valuable and should be accepted because it guarantees [value]." This is your chance to give a final, coherent explanation of your case. If your case is good, then your explanation will be easy to understand and compelling to the judge.

In the last minute tell the judge your voters for why you have one the round. Segue into the last minute of synthesis and analysis by saying, "Now, here are # reasons why the Affirmative case is preferable to the Negative." Then begin listing your voters. For instance, if your opponent's case has any of the V/C relationship fallacies, those should make your list of voters. Here's an example synthesis:

"Voter number one: The Negative's value of justice and criterion of fairness have been shown to be circular. Because they are circular, the criterion does not lead to the value because it is merely a restatement of the value in a different term. In comparison to the Negative's circular value and criterion, I have offered a preferable criterion of Mill's Utilitarianism, and therefore the resolution should be affirmed.

Voter number 2: the Negative's criterion is begging. There is no explanation given for why or when fairness is met, their criterion is in need of another criterion. Because their criterion is essentially another value, and there are no philosophical reasons why fairness relates to the resolution or when and how fairness can be established, their case lacks a real criterion. Because my case offers Mill's Utilitarianism, which is a definite criterion that states exactly when and how my value can be reached, the resolution should be affirmed.

Voter number three: the Affirmative case solves for the Negative values. Because the Negative values justice, but lacks any legitimate criterion, the Affirmative case offers a criterion that not only establishes my value of equality, but also establishes the means for the Negative's value of justice. However, since Mill's Utilitarianism affirms the resolution, the resolution should be affirmed. For these reasons I humbly ask for an Affirmative vote on the ballot."

The more you debate, the more natural this speech will feel. It is the hardest to do well, but it is the most valuable. Keep working on it and it will help you beat out your opponent on those close rounds.

Chapter 6: Flowing

Finally, I am dedicating an entire chapter to "flowing."

For new debaters, "flowing" refers to you keeping track of all of the arguments of the round. It is a form of note taking. I've seen several different methods of flowing, most of which are effective, but more than anything you need to find a system that works for you. You need to find a system that you are comfortable with so that you actually do flow EVERY argument in the round.

Learning to flow is extremely important if you are going to become successful at winning rounds because good flowing is the only way that you are going to have good rebuttal(s) in the round. If you flow well, then you will have a preprepared speech every time you get up to speak in your rebuttal.

Here's how I flow:

I use a blank, white sheet of printer paper, a red pen, and a black pen (black represents the affirmative arguments, and red represents the negative arguments). One side of the paper is labeled as the Affirmative case, and the other side is labeled as the Negative case. For this description, let's assume that you are the Affirmative

Before the round, pre-flow your case taglines down the left column of the sheet with your black pen. When you flow the case taglines, it is good to develop a system of symbols as shorthand. For the value, I write a "V" and circle it, then write the value next to the "V"; for the criterion, I write a "C" and circle it, and write the criterion; for the contention (s) I write "C1," "C2," etc. and circle them. This merely saves time.

If you are the Affirmative, the NC is the first time you will flow. On the Negative side of your flow sheet, (in red ink) write down your opponent's value, criterion, definitions (if any are provided), contention taglines, and sub point taglines (a tagline is a summary phrase attached to a contention or sub point). As you write each, give yourself plenty of room between each item you write down so that you have ample room to write your rebuttals next to them. Spread the taglines of your opponent's case out all the way down (long ways) the left column of the paper keeping it within a half-fingers length from the left edge.

Once your opponent has finished reading her case, they will begin to attack your case. Flip your sheet over and be prepared to write down (still in red ink), her responses to your case value, criterion, and contention. Summarize every one of the arguments so that you will be able to write out responses to each individual argument during your next speech. If an immediate response to one of her rebuttals against your case, or a evident flaw you see in her case pops into your head while your opponent is still speaking, feel free to quickly write your response out next to her point (in black ink, since it's your response) on the flow sheet–then quickly return to flowing her remaining arguments.

Once the speech is over, and after your CX, ask for half of your prep time, and spend the next couple of minutes laboriously going through each point, line-by-line, and writing out (in black ink, now) your response to EVERY argument that you just heard. This way, when you get back up, you will be able to see the line or argumentation from the cases, to the rebuttals, and know what your response is going to be before you even get up to speak.

For each speech, you just write out the next rebuttal, and give your response to it. By the end of the round, you will have a front-and-back sheet that contains everything that was said in the round. This way, you know that you're not dropping any arguments, and it's helpful to be able to look back and review how the round went and identify areas that you can work on and arguments that you could and should have made. Save all of your flowsheets in a folder; you never know when you might here that same case again.

From Classroom to State--Where to Go From Here

Now that you have (hopefully) mastered some of the more difficult aspects of debate such as case-writing, knowing the value/criterion relationship, and learning to flow so you can have good rebuttals, it is time to translate these concepts into the debate room. As I have promised several times throughout the book, if you learn the information that I have included, you will do very, very well. Even by only learning the value/criterion information and how to make convincing arguments based on v/c flaws in your opponent's case, you will automatically be ready to compete at the state level.

But, as I have attempted to stress, this book is as much about *learning how to learn* as it has been about becoming a winner in LD Debate. The "success" that this book is a guide to is not only about being a state champion, winning invitational tournaments, or competing in the Tournament of Champions. For high school debaters, success should also be defined by what kind of student and learner you are becoming and how able you are to engage in healthy dialogue with those with whom you disagree.

Use this book not as a tool to *win*, but as a tool to *learn*. Use it as a jumping off point for becoming a state qualifier, but also as a life-long learner capable of deep thought and reason.

I have done my best to offer a book that is accessible to newcomers to debate, helpful to seasoned debaters, and useful to coaches. If you have further questions, would like to set up a Skype or live workshop, or have any suggestions to how this book could be revised and improved, email me at griffith.ben@att.net.

20642568R00035

Made in the USA
Lexington, KY
13 February 2013